AMAZING MAMMALS

Miles Kelly

PUBLISHING

First published in 2004 by
Miles Kelly Publishing Ltd
Bardfield Centre, Great Bardfield, Essex, CM7 4SL

Copyright © Miles Kelly Publishing Ltd 2004

2 4 6 8 10 9 7 5 3 1

Editorial Director:
Anne Marshall

Senior Editor:
Belinda Gallagher

Editorial Assistant:
Lisa Clayden

Designer:
Debbie Meekcoms

Cartoons:
Mark Davis

Production:
Estela Boulton

ISBN 1–84236–389–1

Printed in China

British Library Cataloguing-in-Publication Data
A catalogue record for this book is available from the British Library

Indexer: Jane Parker

www.mileskelly.net
info@mileskelly.net

Contents

World of mammals
furry beasts

There are nearly 4500 different kinds of mammal. Mammals are warm-blooded animals with fur or hair. A bony skeleton supports the body and protects soft insides like the heart and lungs. Most young develop inside the mother's body. In fact one obvious mammal is you!

Young mammals are fed on their mother's milk. This contains everything they need to grow.

The duck-billed platypus and echidna (spiny anteater) lay eggs instead of giving birth to live young.

Mammals have good senses of sight, hearing and smell. These help to warn them of danger.

Little and large
on land and sea

The blue whale is the biggest mammal, and the largest animal to have ever lived. It measures an amazing 33.5 metres in length – that's as long as seven family cars parked end to end – and weighs a massive 100 tonnes. Although this mammal lives at sea, it comes to the surface to breathe air.

DIRTY RAT!

I MAY LOOK PINK BUT I AIN'T NO PANSY!

HELP!

GLADLY!

LOOK, RATS, MOVE IT! LET ME EAT IN PEACE!

RATS? WE'RE CAPYBARA

The African elephant is the biggest land mammal and a big male can weigh more than 7 tonnes.

The African elephant has the longest nose. Its trunk measures up to 2.5 metres.

The gorilla is the biggest primate. This group of mammals also includes chimpanzees and humans. A full-grown male gorilla is about 1.75 metres tall and can weigh as much as 275 kilograms – the same as four humans. Gorillas live in the rainforests of Africa.

OVER-GROWN RAT...WELL I AM THE BIGGEST RODENT...

ALL THE BETTER TO SEE YOU WITH...

EEEK!

t 5.5 metres giraffes are the tallest animals – this is like four people standing on each other's shoulders!

Flippers and fins
life at sea!

Swimming mammals have flippers and fins instead of legs. Their bodies are sleek and streamlined to help them move through the water with ease. Seals have paddle-like flippers that they use to move about on land as well as in the water. Whales spend all their lives at sea and swim by moving their tails up and down, using their front flippers to steer.

FLIPPIN' HECK!

LOOK OUT FOR KILLER WHALES...

AND SEALS...

CHARMING!

The Weddell seal can dive 600 metres, staying underwater for up to 30 minutes looking for fish.

Not all dolphins live in the sea. River dolphins live in Asia and South America. They feed on fish and shellfish and use a kind of sonar called echolocation to find their prey.

Despite its name, the killer whale is actually the largest member of the dolphin family. It can swim at speeds of up to 55 kilometres an hour, enabling it to catch fast-swimming prey such as seals. A killer whale can be 10 metres in length and weigh almost one tonne.

IT'S YOUR LUCKY DAY — I'VE ALREADY HAD DINNER!

WHAT? HAVEN'T YOU SEEN A SEAL IN A DIVING SUIT BEFORE?

PHEW!

he killer whale is a fierce hunter of seals, fish and even other whales. It hunts in groups in all the oceans.

Fliers and gliders
life on the wing!

Bats are the only true flying mammals. They whiz through the air on wings made of skin, which are supported by the extra-long bones of the arms and fingers. Bats usually hunt at night, spending the day hanging upside down by their feet in a cave or tree. There are more than 950 different kinds of bat.

Bats feed on insects, fruit and small animals. Vampire bats feed on the blood of other mammals.

Other 'flying' mammals can really only glide. These include flying lemurs, flying squirrels and gliders. All these mammals have flaps of skin at the sides of their bodies that act like parachutes.

A vampire bat drinks about 26 litres of blood each year. That's about the total blood supply of five people.

I'M THE KING OF THE SWINGERS!

BOING

IT'S EASY, LIKE RIDING A BIKE...

Flying squirrels glide by stretching out their arms. They live in the forests of North America and Asia.

Cool customers

keeping warm

Mammals can be found in the coldest places. Polar bears live in the freezing Arctic. They are the biggest land predators in the world. These bears are perfectly adapted to the cold, with thick white coats to keep them warm and hairy paws that grip the icy ground.

MY COOL? I NEVER LOSE IT...

KEBAB, TAPAS, INDIAN... ANYTHING BUT MORE SEAL!

Polar bears feed mainly on ringed seals, although they sometimes hunt Arctic hares and reindeer.

A long shaggy coat keeps the musk ox warm. Reindeer spend the summer feeding on the Arctic tundra.

Lemmings dig nests under the snow in winter, while the walrus has blubbery fat to keep out the cold.

Creatures of the night

after sunset...

Some mammals are nocturnal. This means they sleep during the day and are active at night. Bats and owls have the skies to themselves at night – which means there's less competition for food. The same is true of the western tarsier (left), which has huge eyes to help it see in the dark. This mammal lives in the forests of Asia where it hunts for insects.

The red panda of of Asia wakes from its daytime sleep to search for bamboo, shoots and fruit to eat.

Can you believe it?

Foxes often come into city centres at night looking for food. They know that rubbish bins are often full of leftovers that are good to eat.

The red panda is more closely related to a raccoon than a panda. As well as roots and shoots, this mammal eats insects, birds' eggs and small animals. Although mainly a night feeder, in the summer months red pandas sometimes wake up during the day and climb trees to find fresh leaves to eat.

LOOK OUT!

LOOK, WE DON'T WANT YOUR SORT ROUND HERE...

YEAH, RIFLING THROUGH OUR LEFTOVERS...

Hyenas live in Africa, where they scavenge the remains of dead animals at night. They sleep by day.

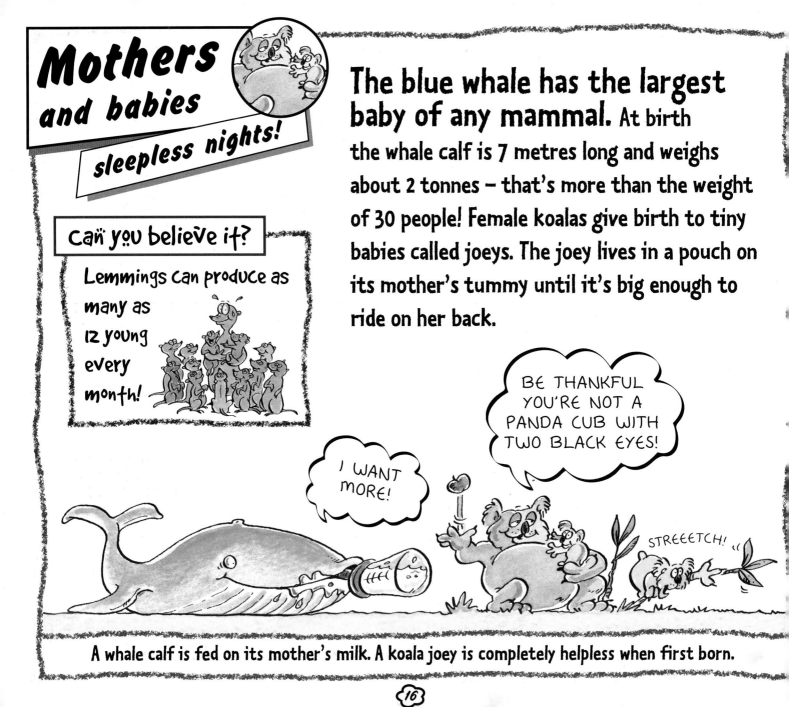

Mothers and babies

sleepless nights!

The blue whale has the largest baby of any mammal. At birth the whale calf is 7 metres long and weighs about 2 tonnes – that's more than the weight of 30 people! Female koalas give birth to tiny babies called joeys. The joey lives in a pouch on its mother's tummy until it's big enough to ride on her back.

Can you believe it?

Lemmings can produce as many as 12 young every month!

I WANT MORE!

BE THANKFUL YOU'RE NOT A PANDA CUB WITH TWO BLACK EYES!

STREEETCH!

A whale calf is fed on its mother's milk. A koala joey is completely helpless when first born.

Some babies, such as antelopes, have to be able to run within an hour of birth to escape hunters.

The Virginia opposum has as many as 21 babies, more than any other mammal!

King of the cats
the Siberian tiger

The beautiful Siberian tiger is the biggest member of the cat family. This huge hunter prowls the snowy lands of eastern Asia. There are less than 200 of these tigers in the wild, making this big cat extremely rare.

The coat of the Siberian tiger is very thick to protect it from the freezing winter conditions. All tigers have yellow, orange or gold fur with black stripes. The Siberian tiger has more white in its coat to help it blend in with the snowy landscape.

Long fur on its cheeks makes the tiger's face look wider

Siberian tigers hunt deer and ox. Usually tigers live alone, but occasionally they'll share a kill.

The tiger is heavily built and weighs about 300 kilograms

Siberian tigers measure 3.5 metres from nose to tail-tip

Females have a litter of cubs every other year. The cubs stay with their mother for at least two years.

Family feuds

staying together

Some mammals live in groups or families. Wolves live in packs of up to 20 animals, chimpanzees live in groups called troops, lions live together in a pride and meerkats live in families of up to 30 animals. Even elephant seals like to live together – males fight rivals to gather a group of females.

Can you believe it?

Lions may be fierce but they're also very lazy. They sleep up to 20 hours every day!

SULK SULK

SCRATCH!

WANNA BE IN MY TROOP?

mmm, DELICIOUS!

I DON'T EAT BANANAS – BUT QUITE FANCY SOME CHIMP...

Chimpanzees' troops number up to 80 animals. Chimps often leave one troop to join another.

A female wolf heads a wolf pack. Meerkats live in colonies and members take turns to be on guard.

Lion cubs are part of a pride, headed by an adult male. A male elephant seal has a harem of females.

Desert dwellers beat the heat!

Many desert animals burrow underground to escape the burning heat. The North African gerbil stays underground all day, coming out at night to feed on seeds and insects. The gerbil is so well adapted to desert life it never needs to drink. All the liquid it needs is in its food.

Camels can go for weeks without drinking. They store fat in their humps as a food reserve.

The red kangaroo is a champion jumper. It lives in the dry desert lands of Australia where it can bound along at 40 kilometres an hour!

Kangaroo rats never drink. Their kidneys are very efficient at controlling the water levels in their bodies, important in dry desert conditions. The kangaroo rat is named because of its long, strong back legs, and the way it jumps like a kangaroo.

CRAB? I'M A SCORPION, YOU FOOL!

GIVE UP THE CHASE, RATTY!

KITTY, US 'ROO RATS NEVER GIVE UP!

Pallas's cat lives in the Gobi Desert of Asia. It has thick fur to keep it warm in winter.

Fangs and fur on the prowl

I COULD KILL FOR A BIG MAC...

Mammals that hunt and eat other animals are called carnivores. Lions, tigers, wolves and dogs are all carnivores. Because meat is such a rich food source, many carnivores do not need to hunt every day. One kill can supply enough food for several days.

ROAAAAR!

LOOK, CAN WE TALK ABOUT THIS LIKE ADULTS?

THERE'S ONLY ONE MORE THING WE CAN DO...

...PRAY?

The tiger is the biggest cat. It creeps up on its prey then pounces, killing it with a bite to the neck.

Bears are carnivorous, but many, except for the polar bear, also eat fruit, nuts and insects. In summer, fish is a favourite food. The bears wade into the water and hook salmon out of the water as they try to swim upstream to lay their eggs.

Polar bears usually eat seals. They stalk their prey, their white coats blending in with the ice and snow.

Forest fever

jungle dramas!

Rainforest mammals live at all levels, from the tallest treetops to the forest floor. Bats fly overhead, monkeys and apes swing through the branches and lower down, forest hunters such as jaguars prowl their way through the undergrowth, looking for their next meal.

TASTY!

YOU FRUIT BAT!

I WOKE UP WITH THIS TERRIBLE RASH. IS IT...

MEASLES...?

I'M THE LOUDEST!

The jaguar lives in the South American rainforest. Pig-like peccaries are among their favourite prey.

The sloth is the slowest animal. It moves at 5 metres a minute in the trees and only 2 metres on the ground!

Sloths are tree-dwelling mammals that hardly ever go down to the ground. The sloth lives hanging from a branch using its hooked claws. It is so well adapted to this way of life that its fur grows downwards, the opposite way to most mammals. This means that rain drips off more easily.

YEP, YOU'RE A BIGMOUTH!

US SLOTHS DO PONG A BIT!

MATE, YOU POSITIVELY HUM!

he howler monkey has the loudest voice in the forest, while tapirs feed on leaves using their long snouts.

Plant munchers
food for all

Plant-eating mammals spend most of their time eating.
This is because plants don't supply as much goodness as meat. A zebra spends half its day eating grass, but at least it doesn't have to hunt for its food like a meat-eating mammal.

G'DAY BOYS!

MUNCH! CHOMP CHOMP!

I CAN HEAR YOU...

YOU ALWAYS HAVE TO SPOIL THINGS!

MUNCH! CHOMP!

Zebras live on the plains of Africa. They are the favourite food of lions, so must always be on the look-o

can you believe it?

Manatees may be the origin of mermaid myths. Sailors may have mistaken these plump sea creatures for mermaids!

The manatee is a slow-moving mammal. It feeds purely on plants that it pulls into its mouth with its large upper lip. These mammals have to eat a lot of plants to support their bulky bodies – they can grow up to 4.5 metres long and weigh up to 600 kilograms.

WHAT YOU DOIN'?

MONKEY BUSINESS!

AN APPLE A DAY...

THAT'S A PEAR.

HALLO SAILOR...

The manatee is a water-living mammal that feeds on weeds. Broad flippers move them through the water.

Fighting back

deadly defences

PUT HIM DOWN!

Some mammals have special ways of defending themselves.
The nine-banded armadillo has plates of bones, like armour, covering its back, sides and head. Its legs and belly are unprotected, but if attacked, the armadillo rolls into a ball. Pangolins (left) are protected from ants that bite by their thick, overlapping scales.

QUICK MATE, ACT LIKE A BALL!

WHERE'D HE GO?

I HATE TO DO THIS, BUT YOU'RE GETTING ON MY NERVES!

GROSS!

Armadillos roll into tight balls if attacked. Skunks spray a foul-smelling fluid to keep enemies away.

Smelly skunks sometimes feed on bees. They roll the bees on the ground to remove their stings before eating them.

A rhinoceros will charge at its enemies at top speed. Generally, these huge animals are peaceful, but a female will fiercely defend her calf. If the calf is threatened, its mother gallops towards the enemy with her head down and lunges with her sharp horns. Few predators will challenge an angry rhino.

CALL ME PINK AGAIN AND YOU'RE DEAD!

QUICK, JUMP ON.

WHICH IS WORSE?

GALLOP!

Sharp spines protect the porcupine while a charging rhino is a scary sight to any animal!

Index